End Geopolitics in 2018

Helga Zepp-LaRouche's Message For the New Year

Dec. 31—This an edited transcript of Helga Zepp-La-Rouche's New Year's greeting, *filmed for the LaRouche Political Action Committee.*

Dear Citizens of the World,

First, let me wish you a good and peaceful New Year 2018. I want to define as the most important goal for 2018, the overcoming of geopolitics. Geopolitics has been the cause of two world wars in the Twentieth Century, and it should be clear to everyone that in the age of thermonuclear weapons, war cannot be a means of conflict resolution any longer. Geopolitics is based on the outdated thinking of Cold War and of a zero-sum game, that is, the idea that if one country wins, the others have to lose. It is simply the wrong idea that it is legitimate to pursue the interest of one nation or a group of nations against the interest of others.

Now fortunately, China has put on the international agenda the new concept of foreign relations, of relations among nations—win-win cooperation to the benefit of all. The reaction to this has been mixed: China has offered this cooperation to the United States and also to European countries. Some nations have reacted enthusiastically, because they see the benefit of cooperation in the field of infrastructure and other areas. For example, Central and Southern Europe have reacted very positively, and many developing countries are on board. Altogether more than 70 countries are already part of this New Paradigm.

But certain others have reacted with hysteria, which is increasing right now, because they see the rise of China, and they know that China has a more successful model, which is more attractive to many countries in the world. They claim that the "China model" is a threat to their democracies.

But maybe the Chinese *are* actually doing something more correctly than these Western democracies. After all, China has moved 700 million people out of poverty, and they have declared that they intend to bring the remaining 42 million poor Chinese out of poverty by 2020. China has even pledged to eliminate poverty worldwide by the year 2050.

Now that means that Europe has to overcome poverty for its 90 million citizens who are living in that condition. The United States has about 42 million. This is absolutely possible *if* they cooperate with the New Silk Road.

One of the biggest challenges for overcoming geopolitics is the outcome of the fight in the United States. There are hearings right now in the Congress, on the unbelievable collusion of the Obama administration, the Hillary Clinton election campaign, the Democratic leadership, and the heads of the secret services of the Obama administration, in cahoots with British intelligence, to steal the election from Trump in 2016. If all of this comes out, and Trump is successful in his efforts to re-establish a decent relationship with Russia and China—which was the first reason for Russia-gate—then, indeed, a new era of civilization can begin.

The cooperation of all nations with the New Silk Road is also the only way that we can prevent a crash of the financial system in 2018, which, if it happens, would be much worse than that of 2008. This will require ending the casino economy in the West, enacting Glass-Steagall banking separation, establishing a credit system, and then, cooperating with such banks as the Asian Infrastructure Investment Bank (AIIB), the New Silk Road Fund and others, to rebuild the real economy.

This is not only important for the United States and Europe, but especially, if we want to reconstruct the Middle East after many years of horrible wars, which were the result of interventionist policies, regime change, and color revolution—then we need to cooperate with China and the New Silk Road to extend that conception to the Middle East.

The *only* way we are going to solve the refugee crisis in a humane way—in a human way—is to cooperate with China in the economic development of all of Africa. If we do that in the coming year, we have the potential for incredible breakthroughs for world peace—but also in the area of science and technology, where, for example, real breakthroughs in the achievement of thermonuclear fusion power are on the horizon. If we succeed in this, we can have energy security and raw materials security.

If we combine all of this with a dialogue of cultures, where each nation represents its own best traditions, so that the others can learn about it, I'm absolutely certain that this will result in greater love for mankind.

There is every reason for optimism for the coming years, because solutions *do* exist. Let us implement them in a decisive way: Have a good year!

EIR Contents

www.larouchepub.com Volume 45, Number 1, January 5, 2018

Cover This Week

U.S. President Trump meets Presidents Putin (above) and Xi (below).

IN 2018

Escaping the Fishbowl

by Robert Ingraham

Dec. 31—The subject of this offering is the prospects before us as we move into 2018, including the necessary changes in policy, in America and Europe, that must be effected if war is to be avoided and peaceful relations achieved among nations in the new year. This urgent question is one of the major themes developed by Helga Zepp-LaRouche in her December 28, 2017 webcast (full text in this issue of *EIR*; video link new-paradigm.schillerinstitute.com), and it is the challenge that must immediately become the highest priority for all persons of good will at this moment in time. We shall briefly recap a few of the salient points made by Mrs. LaRouche, then situate her observations within the context of several events from 2017 which highlight the potential of this moment. Highly relevant observations from Lyndon LaRouche will then be presented, for the purpose of indicating the pathway to victory.

In her webcast, Mrs. LaRouche stresses that 2018 must become the year in which the United States and the nations of Europe give up the outlook of *geopolitics*. This is now a life-and-death issue for all of humanity. She states that, despite the efforts of President Trump to reverse the war dynamic of the 16-year Bush and Obama Presidencies, the neo-cons and neo-liberals are determined to sabotage the Trump initiatives and stick with the image of China and Russia as enemies. They want to continue the British empire geopolitical game of divide and conquer.

Zepp-LaRouche says, "In the almost four and a half years now since Xi Jinping, the President of China, has put the Belt and Road Initiative, the New Silk Road, on the table, there is a dynamic which is unbeliev-able... Well over seventy countries and forty large international associations and institutions are cooperating with the New Silk Road." This is the *New Paradigm*, the era of economic and cultural "win-win" cooperation, a paradigm already in existence and rapidly expanding, and one which can become the global reality in 2018, if the nations of the trans-Atlantic world bury the heritage of British geopolitics once and for all.

Will the world be dragged into conflict and war by the diseased minds who represent the old system, or will 2018 become the year when America and Europe join with the rest of the world in a project for a global economic, scientific, and cultural Renaissance?

The Present Potential

The election of Donald Trump fourteen months ago, and the initiatives of his first year in office, already demonstrate the potential for the needed strategic shift

Donald Trump being sworn in as President, Jan. 20, 2017. Melania Trump (center).

Matt Pottinger, U.S. National Security Council Senior Director for Asia.

President Trump at the Asia-Pacific Economic Cooperation (APEC) Summit with China President Xi Jinping, Nov. 11, 2017.

President Trump signing Space Policy Directive 1, a change in national space policy, providing for a human return to the Moon, to be followed by missions to Mars and beyond.

to occur. During his 2015-2016 campaign, candidate Trump repeatedly called for an end to the "permanent war" policy of the Bush and Obama years. He stated his firm opposition to the policy of "regime change," and he called for an end to the demonization of Russia.

Within weeks of taking office, President Trump ended the Obama policy of overthrowing the government of Syria, and he entered into a limited military cooperation with Russia for the defeat of ISIS in both Syria and Iraq, actions anathema to both the British and the previous White House occupant. Then, beginning in April, he took a series of initiatives. all of which sharply broke with previous U.S. policy:

• On April 6 and 7, President Trump hosted Chinese President Xi Jinping at Mar-a-Lago, Florida, welcoming him to the United States, and beginning an ongoing dialogue with the Chinese leader.

• Trump decided to send a high-level delegation, led by White House adviser Matt Pottinger, to the May 14-15 Belt and Road Forum in Beijing, this despite demands from London and Wall Street to boycott the conference.

• On June 1, President Trump announced that the United States will withdraw from the genocidal Paris Accords on "climate change."

• On Oct. 26, President Trump announced the beginning of a revived War on Drugs. Since that announcement, several significant steps have been taken, particularly to address the murderous opioid crisis now sweeping the nation. This reverses eight years of Barack Obama's implicit endorsement of drug legalization.

• In November President Trump visited China, where he not only deepened his personal relationship with President Xi, but he also signed an agreement for $250 billion of Chinese investments in the U.S.A.

• On Dec. 11, President Trump announced his policy on the Space Program, wherein he signed a new space policy directive to send Americans back to the Moon "for long-term exploration and use," and on to Mars. Again, this represents a 180-degree turn from the Obama policy.

Make no mistake, this is an incipient revolution. The changes that have been initiated are real and profound, not illusory. At the same time, however, adolescent giddiness based on what has been accomplished so far would be a serious mistake. The powers in London and Wall Street, as well as among American neo-cons and neo-liberals, are fiercely determined to stop Trump's policy changes, and the treasonous inquisition of Special Prosecutor Robert Mueller is continuing. One has to look no further than the content of the Dec. 18 National Security Strategy Report—a report which Trump had to personally intervene against to tone down its findings—to witness the depth of anti-Russian and anti-Chinese geopolitics which permeates the U.S. political establishment. It will not abandon this outlook without a fight.

The problem here is that most decent Americans, including many, many self-identified Trump supporters, don't really understand what is going on. Since the inauguration of Harry S Truman in 1945—now 73 years ago—Americans have been born and raised in a culture where imperial geopolitics has been accepted as a "fact of life," an unchallenged axiom of the "way things are." People know nothing different, except perhaps in their hopes and aspirations. At the same time, the monumental, history-changing implications of the Belt and Road Initiative are simply being kept from the American public. Media outlets do not report on it, political leaders denigrate it—and, if raised at all, it is usually portrayed as some sort of "communist plot."

To solve this problem, it is necessary to get at a deeper level of the difficulty.

In its Sept. 17, 2004 issue, *EIR* published an article, authored by Lyndon LaRouche, under the title "Intelligence Organization: How Can Intelligence Serve An Un-Intelligible President?" That article, which addresses the crisis in the intelligence establishment in the wake of the Sept. 11, 2001 attacks, and which includes several specific recommendations for reform, also raises a more fundamental and profound issue, one which is of immediate relevance for solving the problem we face today.

James Fenimore Cooper (1789-1851) in naval uniform.

New York State Historical Assn.

The Necessary Remedy

In fighting to effect policy change, the solution is never to be found in attempting to change "what" people think, nor even in understanding "how" people think. Rather, what is required to bring about a real transformation is to investigate "why" people think in certain ways about critical issues. What are the, usually hidden and unconscious, influences which keep people on a pre-set mental path?

Imagine yourself as a fish, in a watery bowl, lips pressed up against the glass, oblivious to the larger world outside. If you don't understand the deadly evil of British geopolitics, that's the world you inhabit. Your mind, your sense of identity, is prevented from thinking outside of the externally imposed limits which you perceive as "reality."

In his 2004 article, Lyndon LaRouche zeroes in on the need to comprehend this problem of the "fishbowl mentality," what he calls the "electric fences" and self-imposed habituated delusions which restrain people's ability to recognize reality, and lead to errors of judgement and action. LaRouche points directly to the errors of method which flow from faulty axiomatic assumptions, and he demonstrates that there is a fatal flaw in how most Americans understand their own history, including the historic opposition of America to the British Empire.

On strategic matters, LaRouche asks, "What is the Elephant in the Honeymoon Bed" whose existence no one wants to recognize? LaRouche points to the historic role of James Fenimore Cooper and Edgar Allan Poe as the epitome of what a functioning intelligence operation should strive to be. Both Cooper and Poe start from the standpoint of a deep understanding as to the nature and mission of the American Republic. At the same time, both operate from a brutal insight into the nature and intention of the oligarchy. They recognize that the true nature of the strategic reality is one of an ongoing war between two axiomatically opposed systems, two divergent outlooks as to the nature of human society.

The reason why people today are blind to the elephant in their bed is that they live within a post-1945 pro-British culture, one whose axioms they accept as "real," and they wrongly believe that their outlook on the world and society originates within their own minds. Their notion of mankind and the potential future is stunted, like a deformed and malnourished animal. They don't understand human—or American—history.

In addressing the question of "how" people think, LaRouche raises the subject of Fallacy of Composition. He says,

> Fallacy of composition is usually expressed in two categorically distinct ways: (a) Fallacy of composition of selection of category of facts. This includes both the omission of essential categories of facts, and the addition of irrelevant categories of facts. (b) Fallacy of composition of category of principles which define the functional relationship among facts: both exclusion of relevant true principles, or concealment of those principles' employment, or, also, the active or covert addition of false categories of principles into the "equation." It is the second category of fallacy of composition which defines what I have commonly termed "the fishbowl syndrome."

If you don't examine the underlying principles which define what you think, then you will never understand why you think what you think. The defining issue which will determine victory or defeat in 2018 is whether or not growing numbers of citizens, elected officials, and other policy-makers and leaders can make the breakthrough to think outside the fishbowl of British geopolitics.

America's Mission Has Always Been 'Win-Win'

Begin with George Washington's "Farewell Address." Proceed next through John Quincy Adams' Monroe Doctrine, the anti-British Empire policy of Abraham Lincoln, the peace initiatives of Ulysses

Engraving by Phillibrown, from a painting by Alonzo Chappel, 1866

Washington's 1796 Farewell to His Officers.

Grant, the economic development outlook of William McKinley, and Franklin Roosevelt's virulent opposition to colonialism. This is the actual American Patriotic Tradition. Its moral and philosophical roots are in the notion of Man defined by the Declaration of Independence and the Constitution's Preamble. From 1776 to 1945, the underlying Constitutional basis for American policy was distinguished by its opposition to oligarchy, empire and British Geopolitics. During that era, most notably among the best of our Presidents, America's foreign policy was fully coherent with the concept of the "Benefit of the Other," as prescribed in the 1648 Treaty of Westphalia. America's mission was—and must be today—determined by this cooperative spirit.

Lyndon LaRouche has already put forward the path toward economic recovery in his "Four Laws," and LaRouche's remedy is fully coherent with the Belt and Road Initiative. But to get there, Americans are going to have to challenge themselves. The fallacy of composition of principle, the habituated delusion, that must be overcome in 2018 is the acceptance of the oligarchical view of mankind as antagonistic beasts. This is a faulty axiom. Beasts, like oligarchs, fight one another. Humans build a better future. A New World awaits. Seventy nations have already joined. What will America do?

Turn to the East, Not the British Game, Is Our Future—There Is No Turning Back

by Ramasimong Phillip Tsokolibane

Ramasimong Phillip Tsokolibane

The ruling African National Congress (ANC) in South Africa, on Dec. 16, narrowly elected the City of London's candidate, Cyril Ramaphosa, as the party's president. As the ANC's president, he will become the next President of the country if the ANC wins in the Spring 2019 national election. South Africa's current President, Jacob Zuma, was also first president of the party before being elected President of the country for two five-year terms. In December, the contest was between Dr. Nkosazana Dlamini-Zuma of President Zuma's faction, and Ramaphosa. Dlamini-Zuma was the candidate of industrialization and broad, inclusive social advance, while Ramaphosa is best known as the protégé of some of the richest South Africans, most of them white and all of them aligned with the policies and morals of the British imperial speculators of London and New York. Under the South African constitution, Jacob Zuma should remain President of the country until the national elections in 2019

—David Cherry, Jan. 1, 2018

Dec. 24—As the leader of the LaRouche movement in South Africa, I, Ramasimong Phillip Tsokolibane, offer to all patriotic South Africans this special message, appropriate for this season, but especially to those who might lead our nation, both now and in the future. I would have our citizens judge such leaders and would-be leaders against what I say here.

The recent national electoral meeting of the ANC has elected Cyril Ramaphosa as its new president, and therefore presumptive successor to our nation's President, Jacob Zuma. While there has been much commentary about the choice, and the restraints that Mr. Ramaphosa might be placed under by the ANC leadership that has been chosen to surround him in the party, that grouping alone is not what will determine the course of our nation.

President Zuma, who should and must remain in office to finish his term, has responded positively to overtures from the East, especially from the Russians and the Chinese, and has allied our nation with forward-reaching policies of global economic development and prosperity, espoused by those two nations and the BRICS alliance that they formed, of which South Africa became a proud participating member nation.

Under President Zuma's leadership, South Africa has emerged as the leading African representative of the New Economic Paradigm, of which China's global Belt and Road Initiative (BRI) is a leading policy. This emerging new paradigm must replace the decadent and collapsing junk-heap of financial speculation, known as the trans-Atlantic dominated financial system of the International Monetary Fund—Anglo-American empire of money—and policies that bring destruction and death to peoples and nations, including our own nation.

The recent trade and development deals with the Chinese and Russians, created on favorable credit terms, including plans for nuclear energy development at home and participation in the global transportation

South Africa President Jacob Zuma meeting China President Xi Jinping before the Sixth BRICS summit in Fortaleza, Brazil, July 2014.

corridors and network of the BRI, hold the promise of finally freeing Africa from neo-colonial subjugation to the City of London and its Wall Street satrapy, which have held Africa and most of the world in a state of enforced underdevelopment.

This New Economic Paradigm has been the life's work of the greatest American of recent times and the world's leading physical economist, Lyndon LaRouche, and his wife, Helga, known in China and throughout the world as the Silk Road Lady, whose movement I am proud to represent and lead in South Africa. The win-win strategy and proposal of China's President Xi Jinping, supported by Russia's President Vladimir Putin, echo the proposals made over the last more than half century by the LaRouches, rejecting British geopolitics and offering us the only real alternative to the wars and chaos imposed by the collapsing British empire of money.

Only a fool will not realise that for most of his adult life, Mr. Ramaphosa has been a loyal servant of the City of London/Wall Street. His controllers would like nothing better than for him to return South Africa again into their evil grip. But the shift eastward has momentum and is really irreversible, as Mr.

Nelson Mandela
(1918-2013)

Ramaphosa will no doubt discover. There is no hope of solving any of our economic problems outside of the New Paradigm. All attempts to do so will result in the destruction of those who try. Stated another way, our problems were created by our former slavishness to the old, decadent system, and a return to it will produce nothing but disaster, regardless of what Mr. Ramaphosa or his past and would-be current controllers might think or want.

In the coming year, our great nation will assume the rotating chairmanship of the BRICS. Mr. Zuma will host important meetings that will include the Chinese and Russian leaders, including Presidents Xi and Putin. South Africa will assume its rightful leadership—leadership that was the dream and legacy of our beloved father, Nelson Mandela. This new reality is a force far more compelling and more important than either Jacob Zuma or Cyril Ramaphosa. The eyes of the world will find themselves resting intently on what we do now, with our imperfect leaders. The hopes of future generations, yet unborn, will depend on what we do now.

Those future generations will demand, as we must do now, that our leaders rise to the occasion. Mr. Zuma shall lead the way. Mr. Ramaphosa, should he be elected President in the general election in 2019, must follow that lead. The future demands it.

In this season, when we turn our hearts and minds to thoughts of peace and good will towards our fellow men and women, let us commit ourselves to realizing these thoughts by bringing the New Economic Paradigm into being. Thus it is with great hope that I look towards a new year when this beautiful dream can and must be realized. With a hope as great as all of Africa, I look forward to the New Year, and to the New World that must come into being. With my best wishes for the season and for the future, I am,

Ramasimong Phillip Tsokolibane
December 24, 2017

The Key to True Happiness!

by Kesha Rogers

Jan. 1—The great German philosopher Gottfried Leibniz writes in his essay, "On Wisdom," that "Wisdom is nothing other than the science of happiness, that is to say it teaches us to attain happiness."

The pursuit of happiness is the cornerstone principle of the Declaration of Independence. The pursuit of happiness is not the attempt to attain short-term pleasures, or to fulfill sensual needs; rather, it is the recognition of the distinct difference in the nature of mankind from animals. Mankind creates the future we wish to see through our faculty of creative reasoning, powered by the happiness produced by this activity. As President Franklin Roosevelt put it, "Happiness lies not in the mere possession of money; it lies in the joy of achievement, in the thrill of creative effort. The joy and moral stimulation of work no longer must be forgotten in the mad chase of evanescent profits."

This is the true pursuit of happiness. As Leibniz shows, "Nothing serves happiness more than the illumination of the mind and the exercise of the will to act at all times according to Reason, and to seek such illumination especially in the knowledge of things, which can bring our mind always further to a higher light, while from this springs a perpetual progress in Wisdom and Virtue, also consequently in Perfection and Joy, the profit of which also remains with the soul after this life."

As we enter into this new year of 2018, we must define a true mission to fulfill a commitment to the common destiny and progress of all mankind. This principle of the pursuit of happiness is one that belongs not only to one nation, but is an inalienable right of all people and all nations.

In the New Year's message from Helga Zepp-LaRouche which leads this issue of *EIR*, she defines the most important goal of 2018 as the overcoming of geopolitics. Geopolitics has been the destructive agenda of the British empire, aimed to keep people and nations backward and impoverished, and at war with one another in a "winner take all" mentality. Geopolitics is the means of control of the British empire to promote zero growth and economic collapse, through lack of progress, while relying on gambling in speculative markets

The reign of geopolitics has created the poverty, the lack of infrastructure, and the eradication of hope you see here in this NASA composite photo of a space-based view of Earth at night.

for access to money. The rejection of geopolitics is the key to eliminating poverty. Geopolitical economics requires a belief in a speculative monetary system, because it doesn't create true wealth on its own. China has been largely able to fulfill the promise of ending poverty for its citizens by rejecting the destructive trends of geopolitics.

China has been on a total mobilization for poverty alleviation for the last three decades, and has already lifted 700 million Chinese out of poverty. As the President of China relayed in his New Year's message, during the past year China has lifted 10 million more out of poverty. The nation is committed to the total elimination of poverty by the year 2020.

Of the 350 million people living in the United States, there are reportedly 42 million living below the poverty line. But how do we truly alleviate poverty? Is it through tax cuts and stock market spikes? No, there is no simple monetary solution to poverty. Did "the markets" ever plant an acre of farmland, or make a new scientific discovery that contributed to the increase in the physical productivity of the nation? No, these are physical-economic actions, rather than monetary ones.

President John F. Kennedy, in a special address to Congress on Jan. 24, 1963, on "Tax Reduction and Reform," said:

> The most urgent task facing our Nation at home today is to end the tragic waste of unemployment and unused resources—to step up the growth and vigor of our national economy—to increase job and investment opportunities—to improve our productivity—and thereby to strengthen our nation's ability to meet its worldwide commitments for the defense and growth of freedom.

This must be the renewed mission of our nation today. The tax bill just passed by the U.S. Congress does not speak to the effect of ending the tragic waste of unemployment and unused resources. It does not speak to stepping up the growth and vigor of our national economy, or increasing job and investment opportunities. It speaks to none of these solutions, which are more urgently needed for the economic growth of our nation today, than they were over 50 years ago. What this latest tax reform passed by Congress does do, is pump money, not into the real economy, but into more speculation, as did the bailouts and Quantitative Easing.

Eliminating poverty requires an increase in the standard of living of every member of the population, not merely tax-break handouts. It requires the creation of productive jobs, while ensuring that the skill sets of the workforce are increased to meet the demands of work in the creation of new infrastructure, and improvement in the physical economy otherwise. We must ensure not merely the increase in monetary wealth of households, but physical wealth. Elimination of poverty is not solely increasing the dollar income of a household, but providing every household access to transportation, food, and cheap and abundant energy, ensuring that the elderly are cared for and that no one ever has to choose between buying medicine or paying the light bill.

It is now time for the American people to act to demand the creation of a full-scale Federal Credit System to invest in the productive economy. This is the Hamilton/LaRouche model. The full package of Lyndon LaRouche's Four Economic Laws To Save The United States Economy, starting with the reinstatement of Glass-Steagall (as President Trump also supports), must be adopted now. An essential principle laid out in this program, is that "The purpose of the use of a federal credit-system, is to generate high productivity trends in improvement of employment, with the accompanying intention, to increase the physical economic productivity, and the standard of living of the persons and households of the United States." The elimination of poverty in the United States demands that our nation get on board the New Silk Road. America's future on the New Silk Road is the key to joining with the many nations that have dedicated themselves to ending geopolitics, and achieving a shared community of common destiny for the happiness and productive growth of all people. The Fourth Law of LaRouche's economic recovery plan is the adoption of a fusion economy, which, as LaRouche describes, "is the presently urgent next step, and standard, for man's gains of power within the Solar system, and later, beyond."

The development of the resources of our Earth's Moon, is mankind's gateway into the Universe. We must harness the power of the Sun. The mining of Helium-3 on the Moon will unleash access to an abundance of energy to power the Earth for a long time to come. It will give us the means to develop mankind's reach far beyond our Solar system, and to develop plentiful resources to meet the needs of all people, both here on Earth and in our exploration and development of space. This is what it means to unleash the power of creative reason and discovery, which brings about true joy and happiness.

The New Silk Road Is Changing the World: The U.S. Must Join in 2018!

Helga Zepp-LaRouche's Dec. 28, 2017 webcast can be seen at newparadigm.schillerinstitute.com. The transcript has been edited.

Harley Schlanger: Hello—I'm Harley Schlanger with the Schiller Institute. Welcome to this week's Schiller Institute International Webcast with the founder of the Schiller Institutes, who is also the President of the German Schiller Institute, Helga Zepp-LaRouche.

The last weeks have been absolutely full of developments of significant importance, that can be only understood from the standpoint that the Schiller Institute has been presenting. There are the continuing effects of the Mueller investigation, as the neo-cons are attempting to re-emerge; but against that, the great opportunity that's presenting itself because of the tremendous accomplishments in recent months of the Chinese Belt and Road Initiative. And I think, Helga, that's probably the best place to start, because, again, we see the potential if the United States were to join with China—so let's start with that.

Helga Zepp-LaRouche: Yes, it is really amazing: There are two realities in the world. The mainstream media in the West, in the United States and Europe— not all European countries, but some—almost manage to completely ignore that reality, and ensure that the people of the United States and many European coun-

tries don't even know about it. This is a big scandal: What you are referring to is the fact that in the almost four and a half years now since Xi Jinping, the President of China, put the Belt and Road Initiative, the New Silk Road, on the table, we see a dynamic which is unbelievable. First of all, China is economically exploding with development, with optimism, and with very ambitious infrastructure projects—we should talk about that in detail in a minute. Well over 70 countries and 40 large international associations and institutions, are cooperating with the New Silk Road. All of these countries have been gripped by an enormous sense of optimism, which some people call the "Silk Road Spirit," a sense of entering a new era of mankind—while the rest of the Europeans and Americans don't know it! The only people in the United States who have an inkling of it, are those from West Virginia and some other states who travelled with President Trump on his recent China trip, and came back with enormous deals, like West Virginia's MOU for $83 billion over the next 20 years. People really see that the United States could absolutely join and be a part of it.

The key battle in the world, is with the old neo-cons, the neo-liberals, who want to stick with geopolitics. They want to keep the image of China and Russia as enemies, and continue the British empire game of divide and conquer, playing one section against another. Clearly the winning strat-

Presidents Trump and Xi witnessed West Virginia Secretary of Commerce Woody Thrasher and China Energy President Ling Wen sign an MOU between China Energy and the state of West Virginia, as part of the U.S.-China Business Exchange trade mission.

egy is—and that is what Xi Jinping has put on the agenda— "win-win" cooperation of all nations of the world, based on the idea of a new paradigm, a "community for a shared future of mankind," a common destiny, the idea that geopolitics can be overcome. And more and more countries are joining with this new conception.

So, can we get the kinds of changes in the United States in particular, but also in Western Europe, to join in this new paradigm in time, before a new financial crash comes down on us? It's hanging over our heads like a Sword of Damocles. Can we do it in time, or will this battle for civilization be lost? I'm very optimistic it can be won, but it requires activity: This is not a case of dialectical materialism, or historical materialism, where positive events simply take on a life of their own. The *subjective* factor always plays a very large role. One place you can see this very clearly is in the person of Xi Jinping, who has really taken an already positive Chinese development, and given it a complete upgrade, and a complete transformation into a new paradigm. We need people in the West who will do likewise.

The Schiller Institute is absolutely committed to doing everything possible that we can to get the United States and Europe to cooperate with the New Silk Road, because that will be *the* decisive battle for the coming year.

Schlanger: You just mentioned the amazing developments in China, and we can go through some of them, but there were figures that were released just yesterday from I think it was *Global Times*, the Chinese publication, of $350 billion in new investments in China this year. That's on top of what had already been invested as part of the growth of the Belt and Road Initiative, this year with other countries, and these of course are just in one year, and are much larger than that over a number of years. And then the $83 billion for West Virginia, that's almost more than what's been spent in the whole United States, in infrastructure, recently. And you've seen some of these projects, it's really quite amazing.

Zepp-LaRouche: Yes, I think I mentioned how absolutely impressed I was both by the high-speed rail system in China—it's wonderful to travel on trains that go 350 km/h (about 220 mph), with no noise and no

China's 600 km/h maglev train test line expects completion in 2021

(CRI Online) 23:30, November 13, 2016

China's 600 km/h maglev (magnetic levitation) train project, launched earlier this year, is in full swing.

Jia Limin, head of China's high-speed rail innovation program, said a high-speed maglev

China's 600 km/h maglev (magnetic levitation) train project, launched in 2017, is in full swing.

shaking; they're now building a new system which can go 400 km/h, and they're already planning a new maglev train which will go 600 km/h. Then there is the longest sea bridge, between Hong Kong, Macao, and Zhuhai, which is incredible, which I stood on just 15 km away from Hong Kong. This took 120 patents to accomplish, because many engineering and technical problems had to be solved.

I would like to ask you to help us to get that idea of infrastructure development into the United States. There will be a big, important summit on Jan. 6-7 at Camp David, where President Trump will meet with Congressional leaders—Senate Majority Leader Mitch McConnell, House Speaker Paul Ryan and others. The issue will be his infrastructure program for the United States. What has been made known so far, is that he wants to channel $200 billion in Federal money, matched by another $800 billion of local, regional, and state money over the next 10 years.

That is obviously not enough. The White House said this is a "floor, not a ceiling" so that is good to hear, but I think we need a mass movement for development, for infrastructure development, as India's Prime Minister Modi had put it a couple of years ago. Because look at the devastation from the hurricanes in the United States and how slowly it is being repaired: Contrast that with the incredibly ambitious program by China to connect every large city with a high-speed rail system by the year 2020. Beyond that, they will take the entire region of Beijing, Hebei province, and the city of Tianjin, which is an area of 130 million people, and completely transform it through modern infrastructure and relocation of industry—make it more livable for the people. Add an extremely ambitious program to eliminate poverty by the year 2020! By taking very active measures, by building roads into poor, rural areas, and connecting them via Internet to enable them to sell their products through e-commerce—it's just an unbelievable package.

Sen. Black questioned the wisdom of H.R. McMaster's National Security Strategy report.

I was just talking to some of our American friends earlier today. China wants to eliminate all of its poverty by the year 2020—Europe should do the same thing. Europe should have a plan to lift its more than 90 million poor people out of poverty by 2020, and the United States should have a similar plan—I don't know how many people are officially poor in the United States these days, but it must be about 50 million people, so why not say: With such an infrastructure development perspective, all 50 million or so people who are below the poverty line in the United States, could be raised up to a better life. And we need a mobilization for that. Our colleagues in the United States have a new pamphlet, calling for the implementation of the Four Laws of Lyndon LaRouche and for the United States to join the New Silk Road.

So please help us to distribute this pamphlet: Contact us and work with us, because this is not something which will happen by itself, but we need a popular demand for a new paradigm, both in the United States and in Europe.

The Old Curse of Geopolitics

Schlanger: What you just identified gets right to the core of what the fight is in the United States. While it's true that the Trump proposal on infrastructure so far is too small, his intention is to link the United States with the Silk Road—at least that's what he's been talking about. And that's one of the key items that's under attack by the neo-cons in the Mueller investigation. The reason they didn't want Trump in the White House in the first place was because they wanted to continue the old geopolitics.

Now, if you look at this, you come head to head with this new "National Security Strategy"—and we talked about this a little bit last week—as a means of countering Trump's efforts to break with the policies of Bush and Obama. It's worth reviewing the important battle that this demonstrates is under way inside the administration and inside the country.

Zepp-LaRouche: Virginia State Sen. Richard Black gave a very good interview about this National Security Strategy report. He was quite accurate when he said that there was a discrepancy between the report—which was clearly written by the successor of General Michael Flynn as the National Security Advisor, namely H.R. McMaster, or rather some staff around him; and it clearly defines Russia and China as adversaries, as "competitors." And President Trump, when he presented it—in an unusual move, because normally the President himself doesn't present it—clearly used milder language. But there were still too many geopolitical ideas in it—such as the claim that the United States and China are competing in the Indo-Pacific region. That notion, as such, is an expression of geopolitical confrontation against China, which the Chinese media continue to react to very, very strongly, by saying: No, we have offered "win-win" cooperation, and this is the old language of the Cold War, of the zero-sum game.

So it's very important to recognize that while Trump is doing important things, and it clearly still absolutely represents the potential of getting the relationship with Russia and China on a decent basis—the battle really is by the old bureaucracy, so to speak, by the people who are career diplomats, by people who are on lower levels, like the permanent bureaucracy in the different institutions, who have learned nothing but to try to maintain the status quo. Because the status quo in their mind is associated with their privileges and their way of life, and they usually refuse to learn anything new. They're not open to new ideas; they are continuing the Anglo-American unipolar world scheme, which is really the British empire.

The battle really is, can we move in time, the United States and Europe, into a new paradigm, where Russia and China are not looked at as adversaries? Can we really move to the idea of a "joint future for humanity," which is exactly the only way that we can survive?

Schlanger: One area in which we have seen a potential for this change is Syria. There is an upcoming conference in Sochi, Russia, to discuss Syria's reconciliation and reconstruction—reconstruction which involves China's participation. I think Syria is another place where the U.S. can get involved in cooperation with China.

Zepp-LaRouche: Yes, I think this is very important, because at the end of January, for two days there will be a huge conference, a national dialogue for Syria in Sochi, with 1,500 delegates—all the opposition groups except the terrorists from Syria will be there, and naturally the people from the Astana process, including Turkey and Iran. This will be a big conference, and one focus for the two days is on the need for a reconstruction of Syria, going out to the world with an appeal for all countries to join and help in the reconstruction of Syria.

I think this is a very, very important meeting. The week before there will be the Geneva meeting, so I think we will see at the beginning of the year a very hopeful change of the situation in the Middle East; because there is now also a new development for Af-ghanistan. There was a very important meeting of the three foreign ministers of Pakistan, Afghanistan and China, in Beijing, where Wang Yi, the Chinese foreign minister, said the intention is to extend the China Pakistan Economic Corridor, the CPEC, to Afghanistan, to integrate Afghanistan and to rebuild it economically.

So there is a focus on Syria; there is a focus on Afghanistan; and I think these will be important bridge-heads to start reconstructing the entire Middle East. U.S. Secretary of State Tillerson is very much aware of the fact that Syria is one of the areas for U.S.-Russia cooperation in the interests of both. He wrote an op-ed in the *New York Times* recently to this effect. I think it would be a great way for the United States and Russia to consolidate their cooperation by doing exactly that: Reconstruct Syria.

Schlanger: What is happening with the Mueller investigation, which is essentially designed to prevent the U.S.A. from working with Russia and China, and how can this coup attempt against Trump be stopped?

Zepp-LaRouche: One of the more amusing things was a Tweet which President Trump sent out Dec. 26, where he said, "WOW, Dossier is bogus. Clinton Campaign, DNC funded Dossier. FBI CANNOT (after all of this time) VERIFY CLAIMS IN DOSSIER OF RUSSIA/TRUMP COLLUSION. FBI TAINTED. And they used this Crooked Hillary pile of garbage as the basis for going after the Trump Campaign!" It's very good that Trump is intervening in this way, because the fight around Mueller-gate is clearly heating up. There is on the one side, a whole series of conservative Republicans, from congressional offices, from the House and the Senate, pointing out that Mueller is completely biased and therefore should step down; that there must be a complete cleanup of the FBI and the Department of Justice. So there is a growing chorus to this effect.

There is also, clearly, still an ongoing mass media campaign and also there was another campaign—and I think this is crucial—I was thinking about how this recent "me, too" campaign about sexual harassment of women became the most debated issue. I said, "why are they doing this?" Naturally, it is true. I think every woman on the planet knows there is a reality to such behavior. But whenever they play up a big issue like

More of Mueller's lackeys have been subpoenaed by Rep. Nunes' House Intelligence Committee.

that, there's always the question: Why is it being played up right now? One of the victims of this "me, too" campaign was Congressman John Conyers of Detroit, who was accused of sexual harassment, and he had to resign. Conyers was the ranking Democrat on the House Judiciary Committee; that post was taken over by Jerrold Nadler of New York. Conyers has now been replaced as a Detroit Congressman by a woman named Val Demings who, as her first utterance, said that her main priority will be to keep the Mueller investigation going. In such cases, one asks, what is the relationship between bringing some dirt to the fore—and Congress is unfortunately very famous for such behavior—one real political aim was to replace Conyers, who after all has a very important, 50-year-long record of civil rights fights, of being in favor of a decent health delivery system, and many other virtues—replaced by somebody who is clearly there to keep the Mueller investigation going.

This is again a battle which is

Cong. John Conyers (top), forced to resign; Cong. Val Demings (bottom), his replacement on the Judiciary Committee, declared her priority to defend the Mueller investigation.

not yet decided. I think there are many interesting leads in the Congressional hearings. For example, one person who was an assistant to Sen. John McCain (R-AZ) and who was in contact with Christopher Steele, giving McCain the Steele dossier who then gave it to the FBI—has now been subpoenaed by the House Intelligence Committee. His name is David Kramer. And there are many other interesting hearings coming on.

Many people on the side of Mueller, like Rep. Adam Schiff, for example, say this investigation will go on for months because there are hundreds of new witnesses; each witness takes at least three weeks. Then on the other side, people say this is all a waste of taxpayers' money, and it should be shut down immediately.

It's very unclear how this battle will end, but we are asking people to understand that the task-force that went after my husband and his organization in the 1980s and 1990s, the people who covered up 9/11, and the people who are now going after Trump are all the same apparatus. It is really too shortsighted to just call it the "deep state": The "deep state" idea completely leaves out the British angle, which we have documented in a dossier on this affair, which I'm also asking you to get ahold of and help us circulate.

So it's very clearly not decided, but I'm very optimistic that the potential to squash this Muellergate, and get rid of it, so Trump can do his work—that potential is there, but it requires a real mobilization of you and others who want to keep America as a republic and have it join the New Silk Road.

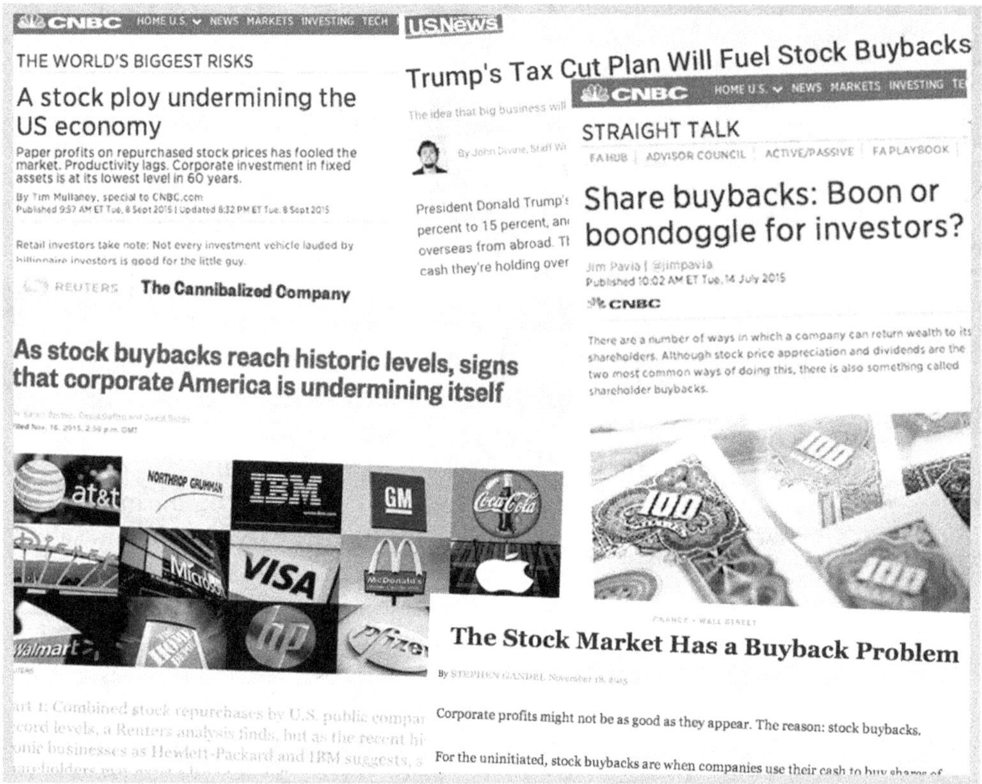

That's what my view is on this matter.

Schlanger: What is your view of the tax bill just signed by President Trump? Will it create jobs?

Zepp-LaRouche: The best way to look at it, is that a tax reduction, as an isolated measure, in the context of the casino economy which is still going on and is threatening the world with a big crash—a tax cut as such does not solve the problem. As a matter of fact, it gives tax breaks for the largest banks and the large corporations, but that does not mean they are going to invest that in the real economy and infrastructure. A good way to look at it, is that last year, U.S. corporations paid altogether $300 billion in taxes, but they were able to invest a half-trillion—$500 billion—into buying up their own stocks, which is a clear manipulation of the market and just doesn't achieve anything, except making the rich richer. I don't think that that is really the solution.

What is needed is nothing less than what my husband, Mr. Lyndon LaRouche, has prescribed: You need a full-fledged return to Glass-Steagall, which President Trump had promised in the election campaign, and so far he has insisted that he is going to keep all of his election promises. So the potential that he will implement Glass-Steagall is absolutely there. It's also clear that Wall Street is trying everything possible to prevent that from happening, but we require a return to Glass-Steagall, exactly as Franklin D. Roosevelt implemented it in 1933, in combination with a National Bank in the tradition of Alexander Hamilton, and a credit system; then cooperation with the New Silk Road: You need this entire package. And you need in particular, in the United States, a Fourth Law of Mr. LaRouche, which is the crash program in high technology to increase the productivity of the labor force.

Again, I always refer to China, as the one country which is doing it in the right way. They're driving an absolute crash program on the development of thermonuclear fusion power. They just announced that they want to build a new fusion test reactor as the successor to the European ITER in France, which will give China the possibility of achieving thermonuclear fusion in the foreseeable future. They also have an extremely ambitious space program.

The United States absolutely needs this kind of increase in productivity through high technology, and an improvement in the productivity of the labor force, and its industrial capacity. If you look at the present labor force in the United States, which is plagued by a drug epidemic, by an opium epidemic, you need really that kind of future orientation to get the kind of spirit which is needed.

So this is the perspective that has to be adopted in the year 2018, because the present status quo is not going to last. I appeal to all of you, use this New Year to get the United States and European countries into the New Silk Road spirit.

October 10, 2008

Why the Economists Failed: Economy & Creativity

by Lyndon H. LaRouche, Jr.

The two items attached to this report, were prominent parts of a discussion conducted, on the subject of the role of creativity in today's crisis-wracked economies. That discussion was conducted among LaRouche PAC (LPAC) and the National Caucus of Labor Committees during this past week of October 7-10. Combined, this piece and the two items copied, below, from the pages of the internal U.S. Daily Briefing of the LaRouche movement,[1] have a crucial bearing on the principles of economy required to resist that general breakdown-crisis of the world economy which has been under way, in fact, since my international, LPAC Webcast of July 25, 2007. That crisis has now entered a most critical, global breakdown phase: it now reverberates world-wide, echoing as that kind of October-November hyper-inflationary breakdown, which struck down Weimar Germany exactly eighty-five years ago, in 1923.

We live, at this moment, in a world which, at this brief instant of its history, had been presently dominated by the approach of the ominous fiscal date of October 10. This already sick world's present financial system, has entered the threatened death-agonies of that present global system of Las Vegas-style gambling, called financial derivatives. The holders of financial derivatives *have* gambled on the virtual race-track called financial speculation, and have lost, and should not be paid off for that. Cancel their worthless "play money" claims; get on, so unhindered, with the business of the

physically real economy of the world. Let the actual people of this planet live, whether Britain's Prince Charles and his batty World Wildlife Fund concur, or not.

The question posed, thus, by this ominous October 10, is: "Where does the world go, from here?"

As I show in this summary report, the only proper response to that present challenge to civilization, is to be found under the heading of scientific creativity, as the proper meaning of that term *creativity* (as distinct from mere innovation) is defined in practice by the development of the original discovery of that principle of gravitation ruling the Solar System. That is a discovery which was made by no one other than Johannes Kepler, a devoted follower of Nicholas of Cusa. As John Maynard Keynes has warned: forget the fraudulent claims of the silly Isaac Newton; close the chest of Newton's wicked and worthless mere arcana! The discovery by Kepler, and no other person, was one more, outstanding triumph in that scientific method of Cardinal Nicholas of Cusa, the Platonic method which a profoundly inspired Cusa had re-introduced to modern European civilization in his **De Docta Ignorantia**.

Now, unless we use that approach to address the present, global economic breakdown-crisis, which grips the world today, there were no hope that our presently menaced global civilization would escape a sudden, deep, and prolonged collapse into a planetary new dark age.

Therefore, our report here proceeds as follows.

Right now, the entire planet is gripped by an accelerating, landslide-like, general, physical breakdown-crisis, a breakdown of not merely those financial mar-

---

1. "Change the Subject," (see page 27) Wednesday, Oct. 8, 2008, and "How the Human Mind Works," (see page 30) Oct. 8, 2008.

National Archive

EIRNS/Stuart Lewis

The silly Isaac Newton (left, portrayed here by Harpo Marx in a 1957 film) embodied the radical empiricist mindset, which makes actual scientific creativity impossible. That mindset caused the current financial meltdown, which the incompetent Treasury Secretary Hank Paulson (right) is failing so miserably to cope with today.

kets which are already hopelessly doomed under current rules. Every part of the world today is now also gripped by a financially-driven, onrushing, but essentially physical, if financially induced, breakdown of the presently crumbling physical means of human existence throughout our planet.

Come back to reality! The present international financial systems can not be rescued! It is now too late for an attempt to rescue those markets themselves; they are far, far gone, and could not be brought back to life in their present form. Our only sane alternative, is to effect the continuity of day-to-day, physical-economic life of the planet, through a process of reorganization in bankruptcy: a reorganization which brings forth a global fixed-exchange-rate credit-system, freed from the carcass of a ruined, lunatic, floating-exchange-rate monetary-system.

It is the physical economy of nations which we must rally to resurrect, and that most urgently, while there are still physically real economies to revive. To bring off that needed rescue, a "Hamiltonian" credit system modeled upon the principle of the U.S. Federal Constitution, must be introduced as the kernel of a global fixed-exchange-rate system modeled upon President Franklin

Roosevelt's 1944 Bretton Woods design.[2]

The crisis which grips the entire world today, is far worse than the crisis from which U.S. President Franklin Roosevelt led the world seventy-five years ago. However, the methods which President Franklin Roosevelt used, while he still lived, saved civilization from a plunge of the planet into a terrible "new dark age," which the sometime pro-Nazi, British and other "free traders" of that time, such as the grandfather of the current U.S. President, would have installed, had they been permitted to do so. The breakdown-crisis today is far worse than that which confronted Franklin Roosevelt, but his outlook and passion could guide us successfully still today.

Your Personal Crisis

Presently, in the case of our United States, the onset of the currently accelerating avalanche of physical-economic decline, should be dated to an accelerating decline of the U.S. economy which began from as far back

---

2. Not the pro-imperialist monetary system which was introduced as a substitute for Roosevelt's intended, anti-imperialist credit system, the pro-imperialist monetary system of John Maynard Keynes, which was introduced under the pro-imperialist admirer of Winston Churchill, President Harry Truman.

as what first emerged as a presently continuing, long-range trend of net physical-economic decline per capita and per square kilometer, since U.S. Fiscal Year 1967-1968. This was the beginning of a continuing net decline in the physical capital of long-term basic economic infrastructure, including highly significant cut-backs in the aerospace investments which had been the greatest factor of increased actual and potential physical productivity of labor at that time. Over the course of the forty intervening years, since the Spring of 1968, since President Nixon's 1971-73 wrecking of the Bretton Woods system, and since the ruin of the internal physical economy of the nation by the evil Trilateral Commission, there has been a continuous process of racheting downward, under one session of the U.S. Congress after another, all leading, as if remorselessly, toward the terrible, global economic catastrophe of now.

Now, under forty years of continuing, year by year, from President to President, of this decline, the net effect of trends in national policy-shaping has been not only the continuation of that failure of policy-shapers, but, there has been a trend of increase of the rate of net physical decline, that, without interruption, over the broad sweep of the four recent decades to date.

Despite the sheepish bleats of our presently hysterical, pompous Pollyannas in party leaderships and government, the principal causes of that forty-year decline should have been obvious to us all. That principal, but excludable factor from among the causes of this decline can be readily located, as follows.

1. A Difference Between Ape and Man

At first glance, it should be astonishing to many citizens, that, it could have been easily and broadly recognized, all along, throughout these forty years of folly: that, the foundation of the wealth of any national economy, and the world economy, depends upon increasing the physical productive powers of labor, per capita and per square kilometer. Yet, very, very few so-called "leading" economists of the Americas and of western and central Europe, have recognized, so far, that there was no possibility for actual success under the reign of what has been, for forty years, those presently continuing, prevalent, and silly theories of economic growth, delusions which were inherent in leading nations' continuing, ruinous policies of national practice of that time.

Any recovery now would depend absolutely on a return to that earlier kind of general increase of the science-driven, physical creativity, upon which any sustained increase in the physical, rather than mere monetary wealth of nations, measured per capita and per square kilometer, depends. This means, especially, an obligatory return to those policies of President Franklin Roosevelt which began to be uprooted by that President Harry Truman who shared some of the imperialist enmities of Winston Churchill, against what had been the actually successful recovery policies of President Franklin Roosevelt.

Similarly, while a significant portion of the economics profession acknowledges some kind of sense, true, or false, of something of the importance of basic economic infrastructure in maintaining the productive powers of labor, most of them today overlook the crucial fact of the matter of the actual role of infrastructure in a viable form of economy. The truth is, that, for science, *this needed benefit occurs, when it occurs, only as it amplifies the productive powers of labor at the point of both production of physical goods, and of the effect of essential services on increases of the physical-productive powers of labor of those employed in science-driven increase of physical productivity at the point of production.*

What is required in the time of today's international breakdown-crisis, is a global de-emphasis on the false doctrine which Karl Marx proudly claimed to have copied as axiomatic from none other than British imperialism's Adam Smith. In fact, it were better to eliminate Adam Smith's poisonous influence entirely, and to replace it with the same Leibnizian principles of the American System of physical economy which the first Treasury Secretary of the United States, Alexander Hamilton, described in his famous three letters to the U.S. Congress. This is the same American System of political economy whose political authority is still, today, implicitly embedded in the practical implications of the anti-Lockean Preamble of the U.S. Federal Constitution.[3]

This American System has a certain history, since its root-origins in the legacy of Plato, and, more recent, modern origins in the role of the great ecumenical

---

3. As to the problems of the U.S. economy since 1968, only a fool would blame the rape-victim for her consequent pregnancy.

Council of Florence, and in the consequent rise of the first model modern nation-state physical economies under France's Louis XI, and Louis' admirer, King Henry VII of England.[4]

Indeed, in the history of the United States, as, still today, the principal English-speaking adversary of the inherently wicked, global, imperialist British system, there is embedded in the founding of our republic, an essential, continuing cultural factor in world history, the factor of our U.S.A. as, at its root, the most efficient opponent of that imperial, Anglo-Dutch Liberal, financier-oligarchical system, the continuing, presently world-hegemonic British financier-oligarchical Empire of 1763-2008. We represent, thus, a U.S.A. for whose continuing role there is still no cultural substitute in history thus far. Without our revival of this factor, this legacy of our United States, it would be impossible to establish the needed, workable, global agreement among nations without which a presently immediate plunge into a prolonged, global "new dark age" could not be avoided now.

Charlemagne (747-814 A.D.), shown here in a painting by Albrecht Dürer, did much to develop the physical economy of Europe. Crucial features of his contributions lived on and helped to shape the later emergence of the Renaissance.

Europe Since Charlemagne

The most urgent political task among nations today, especially the trans-Atlantic ones, is to trace out the most essential elements of those methods of the Augustinians, such as Isidore of Seville, and the kindred predecessors of that Cardinal Nicholas of Cusa, who had brought the spark of what would become the successful expressions of a modern European civilization built upon the form of the great reforms launched by Charlemagne.

Despite the wrecking, after his death, of much of what Charlemagne had done, done by the wrecking by both his own foes of that time, and among those who came after him, the most crucial features of his contributions lived on, as physical improvements and also directions of policy-thinking which would be revived during the founding of modern Europe by Europe's Fifteenth-Century Renaissance of Nicholas of Cusa et al. So, similarly, the United States' constitutional system, forged in resistance to the evil culture of the 1763-2008 Anglo-Dutch financial-oligarchical imperialism, was a resistance which had conveyed its unique accomplishments to serve as the heritage supplied to us by the Council of Florence's mid-Fifteenth-Century Renaissance.[5]

Focus attention, for a moment, on those crucial features of Charlemagne's reforms to which our attention must be turned, in search of remedies for today's crisis, now. Look at the principled role of true economic infrastructure (not the inherently ruinous, Mussolini-modeled frauds tendered by such wicked wretches as Felix Rohatyn, George Soros, and New York's Mayor Bloomberg).

Under Charlemagne and his influence, for example, the greatest increase of the productive powers of labor, per capita and per square kilometer, was achieved through such prominently featured means as the launching of a system of rivers and canals which

---

4. This is either poorly understood, or not at all, among generations born, either here or abroad, since 1945. In the U.S.A., for example, there are virtually no competent professors of history active in U.S. universities today. In their place, we have what are actually more or less honest chroniclers who interpret facts as mere data, and who therefore confuse such exercises with the vastly more profound and serious work of the qualified historian who examines the historical process from a standpoint of reference to the Classical notion of tragedy as a characteristic determination of the course of unfolding processes spanning successive generations. The fact that the U.S. economy has been in an uninterrupted physical decline during each and all of the recent forty years, illustrates the case.

5. The principle of history so expressed is known among theologians as "the simultaneity of eternity." The reference is to the great ecumenical Council of Florence, which celebrated Filippo Brunelleschi's stroke of genius in applying the physical principle of the catenary to craft the cupola of Santa Maria del Fiore.

France's Canal du Midi creates a shortcut between the Atlantic and the Mediterranean. Charlemagne had commissioned a study of the strategic, but difficult, project, as did several other French kings. It was finally built in the 17th Century.

became the principal means of Europe's inland water-borne transport. The role of such systems of rivers and canals was, later, both superseded and assimilated by the development of transcontinental railway systems during the late Nineteenth Century, beginning with that legacy of the Presidency of Abraham Lincoln. Similarly, later, during the period preceding so-called "World War I," Edison's development of the electrical motor, in lovely defiance of the *New York Times* at that moment, resulted in a general increase in productivity in manufacturing, even without comparably significant improvements in the methods of production otherwise.

In the language of the great, Twentieth-Century Russian scientist Academician V.I. Vernadsky, the principal cause of the increase of the productive powers of labor, occurs through situating production and transport of goods and services within that essentially supporting framework of mankind's qualitative improvement of the Biosphere, an improvement which is effected through the qualitative improvement of the Noösphere as such.

The germ of these general benefits to the conditions of life and productivity, **lies within the effect of fundamental discoveries of physical principle, as all such fundamental discoveries are rightly typified by the** **uniquely original discovery of universal gravitation by Johannes Kepler.**

The significance of this most essential feature of any competent view of the physical principles of economy, is made clear, most efficiently, by contrasting the characteristic rates of increase of potential relative population-density of successful forms of society, to the relatively fixed potential relative population-density of either any type of animal species, or of so-called "traditional cultures." The **increase of potential relative population-density of societies**, which is accomplished by the creative powers of the human mind, has no comparable expression within the bounds of the lower forms of life. Man's willful power to increase the "ecological" potential of our human species, is a kind of "ecological" effect which can be compared, among the lower forms of life, only with the processes of anti-entropic, biological evolution.

That, stated in physical-economic terms, is the proper meaning of the term **discovery of universal physical principles**.

The Nature of Creativity

Thus, with the advent of our human species on this planet, a progressive evolution of *human* ecology, has been produced only by the processes of development which are expressed, uniquely, by the creative powers of the individual human mind. In "human ecology," it is the discovery, and adoption of universal physical principles by the individual human mind, and, thus, by society, which is the only competent, anti-entropic, form of human "ecology" available. Any anti-growth human "ecology" is, in and of itself, a tragic failure to perform in the manner appropriate for human beings, and, is a failure which thus serves as the motive for a crime, against humanity generally, such as that of Prince Philip and his World Wildlife Fund.

Mankind is the only willfully creative species known today, excepting only the Creator presented in *Genesis* 1, a Creator whose nature we are instructed, there, to mimic, as that which we are obliged to do according to *Genesis* 1, but which is also an expression of our net knowledge of both the obligation and power of our species. Mankind's normal, healthy distinction as being a higher species, is that of a species which evolves into becoming itself a higher species, with no biological change otherwise, through its self-transformation through the impact of the actual creative powers identified as the discovery and revolutionary application of universal physical principles.

This distinction of man from such as ape and mouse, is what is properly termed *potential human individual creativity*. For whoever might be a competent, present-day economist, the understanding of this principle of specifically human creativity may be located within the modern European, bitter conflict between the followers of Paolo Sarpi and Rene Descartes, on the one side, and, on the opposing side, Cardinal Nicholas of Cusa, and such followers of Cusa as Leonardo da Vinci, Johannes Kepler, and Gottfried Leibniz and Bernhard Riemann.[6]

The issue of that difference is to be identified, categorically, as the ***ontological equivalence*** of Leibniz's concept of the ***ontologically infinitesimal***,[7] that in opposition to the intrinsic incompetence of such adversaries of Leibniz's concept (of the ***universal principle of physical least action***) as de Moivre, D'Alembert, Euler, Lagrange, and of the Nineteenth-Century schools of Cauchy, Clausius, and, later, both the positivist Ernst Mach and the more radical, numerologist form of positivism associated with hoaxsters such as Bertrand Russell and his slavishly perverted devotees Norbert Wiener and John von Neumann.

The latter, same Cartesian form of the moral corruption of the intellect, is typified by all of the known publications on the subject of method of the notorious Adam Smith, a connection shown in the clearest way in despicable Smith's 1759 ***The Theory of Moral Sentiments***.[8]

The significance of my introducing the subject of the aforesaid empiricist miscreants here, is to make clear the issue of the systemic suppression of actual creativity in the pattern of Liberals' behavior respecting scientific matters. Such suppression is typified by that

___

6. I leave the so-called "Scholastics" out of consideration in focussing here on the Cartesian elaboration of the Ockhamite method of the empiricist and other followers of Paolo Sarpi.

7. I.e., rather than the merely mathematical infinitesimal of the empiricists after de Moivre, D'Alembert, Euler, Lagrange, et al.

8. Smith's 1776 anti-American tract, ***The Wealth of Nations***, was, to a large degree, a plagiarism of that work of France's A.R.J. Turgot which was later published in Turgot's ***Reflexions***. This refers to ***The Theory of the Moral Sentiments***, rather than Smith's 1776 anti-American tract, ***The Wealth of Nations***, the latter which is largely cribbed by plagiarist Smith from a too-trusting Turgot's own original, and faulty, work.

assortment of followers of the empiricist method's axiomatic characteristics. My following discussion of this just stated matter of scientific (and anti-scientific) method, will pose difficulties for some readers, just because of the unavoidably scientific nature of the required discussion; but, if anyone is to actually understand competently the implications of the degree of breakdown experienced, internationally, on this date, the subject of these scientific matters can not be avoided.

Before turning to that next chapter, briefly consider the problematic case of Adam Smith.

The Case of Adam Smith

The most significant, persisting cause of tragedies of entire modern cultures, such as that of the present world monetary-financial break-down crisis, is met in the effects of the inherently tragic, culturally hereditary influence of the ban on tolerance for popular creativity among what are usually presumed to be the lower social classes, a ban to be found among sundry varieties of cultures, including that of much of higher education in the U.S.A. and Europe today.

The typical presentation of this idea of such a ban, is that to be found in the tragedian Aeschylus' ***Prometheus Bound***, in which the evil tyrant, the Olympian Zeus, condemns Prometheus to perpetual torture for allowing ordinary human beings to enjoy access to scientific knowledge of the use of that same "fire"which we should associate, today, with such subject-matters as nuclear fission and fusion. Zeus' charge is, that Prometheus has committed that specific offense against the Olympian tyranny, of revealing the secret of man's use of fire, such as nuclear power, to the Olympians' serf-like subjects, the ordinary human beings.[9]

Adam Smith's theory of society, his ***Theory of the Moral Sentiments***, on which his economics dogma is entirely premised, reflects not only the same doctrine of rule by the Olympian Zeus of the ***Prometheus Bound***, but also that dogma of the medieval irrationalist William of Ockham on whom the Venetian reformer Paolo Sarpi had premised what was to become the characteristic Liberal dogma of the modern, Anglo-Dutch Liberal system.[10]

European civilization has had a foretaste of this type

___

9. So, it were proper to think of the anti-nuclear "environmentalists" of today as "Satan's mass-murderous, slimy little helpers."

10. For pedagogical reasons, I have reserved the treatment of this crucially significant connection to a place in the report below.

of force of tragedy exerted across the span of successive generations of a culture, in the relationship of the Homeric argument of the *Iliad*, to the common, subsumed subject of what are called, today, ancient, Classical Greek tragedies.

The individual in history, as portrayed in the *Iliad* and its echoes in later Greek tragedy, is not, in reality, a Cartesian-like building-block; rather, the individual is an expression of a truly dynamic process, as the ancient Pythagoreans and Plato employed the notion of a scientific method premised on the same dynamics (e.g., *dynamis*) affirmed by Gottfried Leibniz, that against the fraud inherent in the method of Rene Descartes, and also against that reductionist method of Paolo Sarpi and his follower the Cartesian Antonio Conti, and also Conti's followers, such as the neo-Cartesian Isaac Newton, Voltaire, de Moivre, D'Alembert, Euler, Lagrange, Laplace, Cauchy, Clausius, et al.

Having said that much on this matter thus far, if we are to actually understand the root of the crucial issues of world economy today, we must set forth the two, respectively distinct, but interrelated issues which flow from the conflict of the scientific method of Cusa, Leonardo da Vinci, Kepler, Fermat, and Leibniz against the methods of both the medieval Aristoteleans and the followers of that doctrine of that medieval figure, William of Ockham, whose intellectual model was adopted by the Paolo Sarpi from whom the modern Liberal philosophy of post-February 1763 Anglo-Dutch imperialism was derived, from that time, to the present day's world crisis.

The first of these issues is the modern method of competent physical science, a method derived, largely through the modern intervention by Nicholas of Cusa in his *De Docta Ignorantia*, but echoing the ancient scientific method of the Pythagoreans and Plato.

2. On The Subject of Human Creativity

The follower of the dogma of Aristotle, Euclid, had worked to destroy the Classical science of his time, by co-opting, and reworking theorems developed by more competent and honest earlier discoverers, into a scheme under which all of that earlier knowledge was reified to conform to the a-priori presumptions which Euclid employed as definitions, axioms, and postulates. The fraud of Euclid's method was employed by the Roman era's hoaxster, Claudius Ptolemy, for crafting an intentionally fraudulent representation of Classical Greek astronomy.

A new version of a similar reification of practical knowledge was introduced to modern European culture through the adoption of a more wildly irrationalist scheme associated with the medieval figure of William of Ockham. This scheme was adopted, and promulgated by the new Venetian faction of Paolo Sarpi and by Sarpi's lackey Galileo Galilei. The result of this became what is known as empiricism and its derivatives, such as positivism, today.

The intention underlying Sarpi's role in this matter, was twofold. First, to provide the Venetian faction with a rationale for allowing some forms of technological innovation which the Aristotelean dogma of that time forbade, but without permitting the subject of the actually creative processes of the human mind to come into play. This so-called empiricist dogma of Sarpi, Galileo, Rene Descartes, Antonio Conti, et al., provided the basis for what John Maynard Keynes was to expose later as the morbid hoax of "black magic" speculator Isaac Newton.

The key to understanding the effect of this dogma of Sarpi on physical science and economic practices, is found in the fact, that the common characteristic of ancient Euclidean dogma and the new, modern Sarpian dogma of empiricism, is *the exclusion of consideration of actually universal physical and comparable principles* through the device of adoption of exclusionary a-priori assumptions such as those of Euclid and Descartes, respectively. Instead of discovering actually universal physical principles, as this is illustrated by the work of Johannes Kepler, the empiricists substituted a form of description known as a mathematical formula, or something comparable, even an outrageously wild hoax, such as the mechanistic positivism of Ernst Mach and his follower Ludwig Boltzmann, or the wildly insane numerology of Bertrand Russell's *Principia Mathematica*, and such of its derivatives as the hoaxes of Russell devotees Norbert Wiener and John von Neumann, instead of an actual physical principle of nature.

To understand the modern positivism of the likes of Mach's and Russell's devotees, it is useful to compare these with the devices and effects of the earlier Euclidean hoax.

In both types of cases, the place which should be occupied by experimentally validated discoveries of universal principle, is occupied by arbitrary appeals to the popularity of the idea of sense-perception as a substitute for reality. In ancient Euclidean modalities, the definitions, axioms, and postulates are assigned this function. In the case of Sarpi's empiricism, the crafting of a convincing composition of arbitrary presumptions became a more complicated undertaking. The result of the latter problem was the mystical doctrine of a-priori forms, on which the fraudulent mathematics of Descartes was grounded. All generally adopted modern empiricism and its derivatives are premised on Descartes' underlying notions of an a-priori roster of forms.

In turn, then, Descartes and his devotees, such as Conti, Voltaire, de Moivre, D'Alembert, Leonhard Euler, and Euler protege Joseph Louis Lagrange, emerged as the principle devotees of a Sarpian, anti-Leibniz cult of empiricism, of which the neo-Cartesian, allegedly Newtonian, British school of empiricism was merely a derived trademark. The "begats" of that breed are as amusing as any popular comic page to read, but few among such readers actually know anything important about what they pride themselves in appearing "to talk about" in a mockery of a learned dialogue.

The essential feature of Sarpian empiricism is brought to the fore, after Sarpi's lackey Galileo, by Descartes, whose mathematical dogmas are merely a projection, from Descartes' reduction of modern empiricism, to a system of a-priori mathematical forms.

In both cases, that of Euclid and Descartes, the subject of deliberation is a set of a-priori mathematical forms, forms which are attributed to sense-perception, not actually physical principles. In the case of Descartes, for example, knowledge is limited, as a possibility, as a matter of a set of a-priori, quasi-sense-perceptual forms. The explicit argument by Descartes, who echoes the Euclideans that far, is that man's knowledge of the universe is limited to such a set of a-priori forms. In this, Descartes imitates the swindle of Euclid and the Euclideans; both schools assume that an impenetrable barrier exists, separating this side of the experience of such forms, which was presumed to be correct, but prohibiting the human mind's access to the underlying reality which exists only on the other side of sense-perception, a side which the empiricists deemed inaccessible to human mental experience.

The distinction which I have just underlined in that manner, is between science as defined by both the ancient Pythagoreans and Plato, on the one side, which locates the experience of perception as merely the shadow cast by the instruments of our sense-perceptual powers, as distinct from the standpoint of those experimentally discoverable universal principles which have cast the shadows which we may recognize as merely sense-perceptions. The power of human creativity which distinguishes human powers absolutely from those of beasts, is the basis for the systematic knowledge given to us from the ancient Pythagoreans and Plato, and of modern European physical science since the fundamental discoveries in science by Nicholas of Cusa and such among his followers as Luca Pacioli, Leonardo da Vinci, Johannes Kepler, Fermat, Leibniz, Bernhard Riemann, and such Twentieth-Century moderns as Max Planck and Albert Einstein.

The complementary feature of this distinction is that the actual comprehension of universal physical, and of equivalent principles, actually exists only as the actually efficient substance on the ontologically "other side," opposite to sense-perception. The corollary point, as to truth, is that no actual universal physical principles exist, ontologically, within the domain of sense-perception as such. Universal physical principles exist only as experimentally definable, efficient universals. This definition is best illustrated for the modern classroom, by the way in which Kepler presents the discovery of universal gravitation in his *Harmonies*, as that which is neither the perception of sight or (harmonic) sound, but is made apparent by the ontological contradiction projected as by the experimental coincidence of the two.

The result of such true discoveries of efficiently universal physical principles, expresses that power of efficient discovery of actually universal physical principles which is specific to the human individual among all known living species.

The Subject of Immortality

Thus, Kepler's account of the problem of defining a principle of universal gravitation reigning in the Solar System as a whole, brings our attention to the related point made by Albert Einstein, and, in that way, makes clear the actual meaning of the *infinitesimal*, as that latter term is defined and employed by Gottfried Leibniz. The discussion of this connection of the work of Kepler follower Leibniz to Einstein's appreciation of Kepler, defines the proper use of the term "infinitesimal" in the practice of physical science.

"Infinitesimal," employed as a term in that context, is not what the hoaxster Leonhard Euler alleges, fraudulently, to be "smallness in space-time." The relative smallness of an interval of action in a gravitational field is actually the relationship of the size of the universe defined by the principle of universal gravitation, relative to any degree of smallness or brevity of the observed part of the local action one has chosen to measure. In that sense, and only in that sense, the smallness of the chosen interval of action considered, is a reflection of the fact that the principle encloses the universe in the manner which Einstein emphasizes as characteristic of a universe which is finite, but unbounded by any efficient external consideration.

All competently defined notions of universal physical principle present us with the same irony which Einstein recognized in Kepler's founding of the only valid approach to the founding of a universal, experimental physical science.

Thus, in Leibniz's (and also Einstein's) rejection of a Cartesian manifold, the universe is not defined by unknowable forms sealing off the mind from that which is not merely sense-perception. It is the discovery of universal physical principles which bound the universe, with respect to some principle, as Einstein states that case for the universe as a system in the likeness of the portrait of physical processes provided by Kepler's discovery of universal gravitation.

It is through that method of discovery, the method traced from the ancient Pythgoreans and Plato, through the fundamental discoveries of Nicholas of Cusa and his followers among the leaders of valid modern European science, that man transforms what Vernadsky defined as the Noösphere, as if from the top, down, thus creating the general environment within which individual human action for change is situated.

It is only the mind whose approach to economy is physical, rather than financial accounting practices, which is capable of understanding, and accounting for the relative values generated by economic processes.

The summation of the progress of mankind thus far, is associated with the work of Bernhard Riemann, a Riemann to be considered as Einstein did, in his department of work, and as I have done in mine. For both of these approaches, a certain essential result is the same: the revolutionizing of human practice of society through the nurture of the creative powers of discovery uniquely specific to the human mind. Progress is not the fruit of habits, but of revolutions in habits of society as a whole, as I have indicated in the memoranda featured in the leads of the briefings for this past Wednesday and Thursday.

Change the Subject

by Dennis Small, *EIR* Editorial Board

The following appeared in the Wednesday, Oct. 8, 2008 edition of the internal daily briefing of the LaRouche political movement. See Lyndon LaRouche's comments following this article, on page 30. Subheads have been added.

We are in the process of making another three or four revolutions, Lyndon LaRouche reported to the Tuesday night, Oct. 7 gathering of the LYM (LaRouche Youth Movement) and NEC (National Executive Committee) of the LaRouche political movement. The recent music work in Boston, and new breakthroughs by our "Basement" science team around Kepler and on the Riemann project, are at the center of the process.

The key problem the world is now facing in the economic meltdown crisis, Lyn began, is conceptual. Almost no one has any understanding of actual physical science anymore, and yet, this is the basic problem of modern civilization. Few Baby Boomers ever really got into the subject at all, and although we approached the subject with the LYM's Kepler Project, we never really resolved it. To address the matter, let's first establish the historical context.

The attempt to overturn the achievements of the 1439 Council of Florence came to the fore with the 1492 Expulsion of the Jews from Spain. We had a period of religious war outbursts that raged throughout Europe, from 1492 up until the 1648 Peace of Westphalia. Machiavelli explained the central issue clearly: The Habsburg reactionary pigs couldn't entirely suppress the Renaissance with their methods, and so the Venetian Paoli Sarpi (1552-1623) emerged, with ideas that were not all that original, but which shifted the approach, and relocated the center of the operation to the North.

Recall that the big North-South division of Europe began when the Venetians sent Henry VIII a marriage counselor. At the Council of Trent (1545-1563), Machiavelli's point was in fact acknowledged, which is that the Renaissance had introduced a cultural change in the cities of Europe, a shift from the old guilds to the new artisanry, which meant that these layers, organized as military forces, could defend the cities and prevent the Habsburgs from winning. The Habsburgs could launch bloody religious warfare across Europe, but they couldn't *win*.

So, Machiavelli emerged as a great thinker, as the founder of modern military science, as a necessary touchstone of all European military training up to the present.

Faced with this problem, Sarpi—who was against Aristotle and smarter than him, although with the same underlying philosophy—got rid of Aristotle, because that approach, as embodied in the Habsburgs, had failed to destroy the Renaissance. Sarpi instead revived the degenerate lunatic William of Ockham (1285-1347) as a paradigm, a paradigm whose name is *Liberalism.*

Sarpi's Ockhamite approach was radically hedonist, based on the axiom that sense certainty rules in all domains. There is no truth, no underlying principles, only what sense certainty teaches by way of information. Therefore, he argued, technological innovation is okay, but *not truth*, not principles.

It is because of this disease of *Liberalism* that the conception of principle virtually no longer exists in modern European civilization.

The Great Issue Today

This is the fight today. The systemic difference between the European and the American systems, both in economics and politics, is the difference between social conventions, on the one hand, and the Presidential system, on the other. It is the difference between a system under which currency is uttered by the government *only*, and the European model of monetary system, in which private interests are allowed to utter. Since those private interests are enemies of the nation-state, and are global, the essence of a monetary system is supranational by nature.

This is the great issue today, Lyn explained. There are quadrillions of dollars of debt running amok in the world, fabricated by private financial interests, which cannot be paid. If we reorganize the system, and put it into bankruptcy reorganization in order to avoid collapse, we will have to eliminate 80% or more of the "money" or debt now circulating. We will have to wipe it out, *burn* it—even if it's in some people's pockets.

Face it: This is a money-oriented culture. People relate to each other and themselves around money. "You got money? I got money? She got money?" This is our problem in science, and in culture.

The way we address this is with the following thesis: There is no such thing as a mathematical statement of *principle*. The very idea of "science based on mathematics" is utter nonsense—an oxymoron liberally peddled by Sarpi. No universal principle can ever be represented by a mathematical formula, and to think that it can, is idiocy and incompetence.

Just take the case of Isaac Newton (1643-1727), that piece of crap. Newton is the standard at universities today—the idea that mathematical formulas can represent reality. Anyone subjected to such university education has absolutely no understanding of physical science. And the real tragedy, is that *people don't know that.*

If you think through the concept of the infinitesimal, the idea becomes clear. On the one hand, you have sense perception. You experience the universe through your senses, such as hearing, and vision. In hearing, you know only harmonics: Any attempt to linearize hearing, or to represent hearing linearly as vision, does not work. The way to think about it is that we are equipped with two primary sensory devices: sight and hearing, and there is absolutely no ontological similarity between them.

Johannes Kepler (1571-1630) understood this. To determine the orbits of the planets, he looked at the entire planetary *system*, not a single orbit. Because the orbit is not defined by itself. What orders it? The planetary system of which it is a part. So Kepler used vision as the basis of his first attempt. But he was able to solve the problem of the ordering of the orbits based on discoveries under the influence of Cusa and Leonardo da Vinci (1452-1519), with the Platonic solids—with the *idea* of the solids, with the root concept. There is absolutely no explanation for this within the domain of vision alone. So he went to *harmonics*, which produced his discovery of the universal principle of gravitation.

So, as with Kepler, what we know is *not* based on sense certainty. Sense certainty is a fraud. Take the example of microphysics: the senses don't work at this level. You have to infer the ordering in the domain by *harmonics*: you cannot linearize. What you can do is create instruments which act like artificial senses. Then you have to ask: Is this sense-certainty true? No, it is not.

What Is Truth?

What is truth? It is the function of the mind in discovering the real meaning of the disinformation coming from sense certainty. Cusa, Plato, the Pythagoreans all knew this: that the location of knowledge lies not in practical experience, but in the paradox of harmonics and vision, and your mental activity to resolve that paradox.

All education on this subject in our culture has been crap. The issue is the *mind*, not the *senses*. Only in and through the *mind* can you know truth. All competent science agrees with me on this, Lyndon LaRouche stated.

So the problem that we have, both in ourselves and as organizers, in understanding economic and social processes, is that we have been brainwashed: Kinetic interaction is presented as cause-and-effect. And we don't look at the actual reality of life today.

What is that reality? For the lower 80% of income brackets, for the majority of the world, they are facing a system that is clinically insane. *Everything* is coming down. Like this crazy bailout bill which was just passed by Congress. It is utterly insane, as are the hyperinflationary policies that have followed it, day by day.

Incompetence, on the other hand, is what you get, including among our own people, when people believe what the press tells them, when they adapt to social processes around them, when they bend their knee to what all "experienced" people tell them. "Experience teaches us this. Experience teaches us that." You've all heard it. So you should say: "Oh, yeah? Your experience hasn't performed too well in this crisis, has it?"

Instead, many of our own Baby Boomers will try to confuse people with a lengthy litany. Because they have been educated in *Liberalism*, they don't believe in truth, and they try instead to create a *belief* in others, to get them to agree to share their *belief*—rather than have a short conversation about reality. And so they sound like liberals—which is what the population most hates! And you wonder why they hang up on you?!

The Real Meaning of Tragedy

The way to make a revolution is by going *against* the idiots who are refusing to recognize this reality. The U.S. economy, in physical fact, has had no real growth since 1967-68. The *tragedy*—and real tragedy always applies to a society, not to the individual—is that people actually believe that there has been growth under this system. It's like the guy who drives his truck right into a tree: You have to say, "Boy, that was crazy." Well, when an entire society does the same thing, as it is doing now, you have to say: "This is crazy."

To avoid tragedy, societies need individual *leaders* to go against popular opinion. It is the fear of going against popular opinion that is always a disaster, corruption. For example, people don't believe in the *human soul*. They believe they *are* their senses while they are alive. But your actual life does not end; your influence lives on beyond you in the mental powers of others. Most people lack that sense of purpose in their lives. Once you die, your senses are gone; the importance of life is what you contribute with it. You need that *intention* in life in order to outlive your own last breath.

The universe is composed of just such universal physical principles, which are beyond the bounds of sense perception. The most obvious of these is your life. People imprison themselves by confining themselves inside society. Tragedy is when there is a lack of a leader to lead from *outside* today's society, to help people break free from their own imprisonment.

So, don't adapt to what the enemy does. Always address the horrors of the crisis facing society, but then immediately switch to something that is intellectually uplifting.

Change the subject!

Never do what you tipped the enemy off to expect you to do. Get his nose pointed in that direction—and then kick him in the ass! Hit him with what he thinks is irrelevant, with what he doesn't undestand. Ridicule him! Outwit him!

People tend to go in straight lines. Instead, *change the subject!* Hit him on another issue, and do it with humor. And as you practice doing this, you will develop your own creativity.

We are a small organization, and we have to move fast to succeed. So, change the subject.

How the Human Mind Works
(The Sight & Sound of Science)

by Lyndon H. LaRouche, Jr.
October 8, 2008

The following subject-matter, omitted from Dennis Small's report (see above, page 27), should be added to the reading of Small's report.

The most crucial of the issues posed by the present, world-wide, physical breakdown-crisis of the present world monetary-financial systems, is the factor of the suppression of the recognition of the role of human individual creativity in determining the relative physical productivity of labor in economies, as measured in physical terms, per capita and per square kilometer.

The point to be emphasized, is that virtually no secondary or university student graduated since approximately 1968, has any actual, mere comprehension of what scientific and related creativity actually signifies in practice. This problem is most notable in those students who mistake mathematics-at-the-blackboard for physics. Thus, the emergence of the role of actual creativity within the work of the LaRouche Youth Movement (LYM), especially the "basement operations," is of the greatest significance for treating the crisis which menaces all of mankind at the present moment.

In the context so identified, it is, therefore, of the most notable relevance, to focus attention on the fact that the presently customary reliance on Liberalism's notion of statistical determination in measurement and forecasting of net performance of economies excludes any competent notion of human creativity in the most thoroughly vicious manner. Hence, the intrinsic incompetence, respecting long-range forecasting of all among my known rivals, including would-be rivals in my own association.

Notably, the errors, on this account, which I have been forced, implicitly, repeatedly, to counter among my own associates, are often a result of their attempting to propitiate commonplace opinions met within sundry strata of the population, especially a morally rotten leading press, such as the ideologies of the *Washington Post* or *New York Times*.

Similarly, we have, also, the ideological pressures upon my associates which reflect both the intrinsically anti-scientific bent of the so-called "Baby Boomer" generation's influence inside the Congress, as elsewhere. This includes the phenomena of the peer pressures on my own immediate associates from the population in general. These combined, intellectually and morally corrupting outside influences on our work, must be recognized as representing a broader, pervasive, systemically tragic factor controlling the mass-behavior of nations and their populations thus far.

It is the influence of those corrupting beliefs which has been the most significant of the efficient political forces causing the present, global breakdown-crisis of not only the U.S.A., the Americas, and Europe generally.

The Rot Called 'Liberalism'

As we must emphasize in this specific kind of discussion, the general cause for the tendency for the breakdown-crises known to the history of European culture and its nearby antecedents, is that identified by the historian-dramatist Aeschylus' ***Prometheus Bound***: the prohibition of knowledge of the principles of scientific-economic creativity (e.g., "fire") by the legendary Olympian Zeus. In all known empires, including Rome and later, as in the Babylonian tradition earlier, the general suppression of the creativity of the great majority of the population, is the characteristic root of all the major evils, and consequent doom, of what had been once powerful cultures.

As I emphasized, once again, in last evening's briefing-session, the systemic failures in modern European physical science and economy, have been chiefly the consequence of the introduction of what has become known as the Anglo-Dutch "Liberalism" which Paolo Sarpi premised on the lunatic method of the

> **The point to be emphasized, is that virtually no secondary or university student graduated since approximately 1968, has any actual, mere comprehension of what scientific and related creativity actually signifies in practice.**

medieval William of Ockham (Occam), which has been the principal source of the lunatic corruption expressed within Liberal reflections on subjects of modern physical science and social practice generally.

Most notably, it has been the figures of René Descartes and his bastard offspring, the largely mythical Isaac Newton, which has been the most vicious of the destructive forces within the teaching and practice of modern science, and also the axiomatic root of the inherently destructive nature of the misanthropic notion of political economy associated with imperialist Lord Shelburne's lackey Adam Smith. There is no science worthy of that name in any aspect of notions of economy traced from the syphilis-like influence, and the filthy sporrans, of David Hume and Adam Smith.

As I emphasized, again, during last evening's meeting, to find a competent trace of the spoor of that foul perversion known as modern European, Anglo-Dutch Liberalism, we must view that Venetian pervert known as Paolo Sarpi, against the backdrop of the earlier activity of the circles of Venice's Francesco Zorzi (a.k.a. "Giorgi") as marriage-counsellor to England's King Henry VIII. The essential features of the account run as follows.

The medieval system of rule by a Norman chivalry which was itself, in turn, controlled by the Venetian financier-oligarchy's Lombard investment-banking system, broke apart in the Fourteenth-Century collapse of Europe into a New Dark Age. The later happy outcome of what had been this disastrous European crisis, was the founding of a modern European civilization through events converging on the great ecumenical Council of Florence.[1] The Venetian reaction against that great Renaissance was expressed most significantly in events beginning with the orchestrated fall of Constantinople and immediately subsequent developments. The rise of Venetian power, which followed as a consequence of the fall of Constantinople, led into the vast religious warfare, of 1492-1648, which began with the expulsion of the Jews from Spain.

The efforts of the Venetians and their Habsburg puppets, to crush the effects of the Renaissance, ran into the growing strength of the modern nation-state, a growth typified by Louis XI's France and Henry VII's England, which were concretized expressions of the work of the Renaissance. This conflict between the forces of the Venetian-controlled Habsburg party and the legacy of the Renaissance principle of the modern nation-state system, prompted the Venetian party's efforts to divide Europe

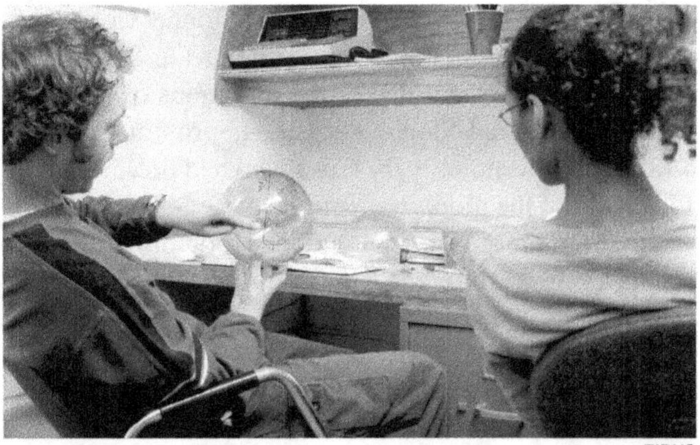

EIRNS

Peter Martinson and Tarrajna Dorsey, members of the 2007 Basement Team, work on spherical geometry. "The emergence of the role of actual creativity within the work of the LaRouche Youth Movement," wrote LaRouche, "especially the 'basement operations,' is of the greatest significance for treating the crisis which menaces all of mankind at the present moment."

between two conflicted parties. This division was built up by Venice's corruption and control, by Zorzi, Cardinal Pole, Thomas Cromwell, et al., of the manifestly insane Henry VIII, a division, brought about by the defection of Henry VIII, which split Europe, to the present day, between, principally, a nominally Catholic, Habsburg, and Protestant parts. Hence, the religious warfare of 1492-1648, which historian Friedrich Schiller described as men fighting one another, not as men, but as beasts.

During this interval, the outcomes of the 1542-1563 Council of Trent, were the interdependent relationship between that Council itself and the rise to power of the Venetian faction of Paolo Sarpi. Sarpi continued the trend which had been set into motion, earlier, by Zorzi's role as marriage counsellor to what became, under his influence, England's lunatic butcher Henry VIII.

The immediate effects of this new division of Europe against itself, persisted as a Venice-directed religious warfare until that 1648 adoption of the Peace of Westphalia with which a decent quality of European civilization became a possibility again, but, as Gottfried Leibniz emphasized, with the highly problematic, persisting division of Protestant from Catholic parts.

However, the 1648 defeat of the cause of religious warfare, while setting back the Habsburg interest, left the emerging superior power of northern maritime Europe in the hands of the essentially evil, Liberal followers of Paolo Sarpi.

Our U.S. Legacy

To identify the significance of the creation of our U.S.A., we must return our intention to its essential ori-

---

1. See William F. Wertz, Jr., *Toward a New Council of Florence* (Washington, D.C.: Schiller Institute, Inc., 1993), Introduction: pp. 1-55.

gins, with attention to the work of Christopher Columbus.

Columbus, a Genoese navigator in the Portuguese service, become informed of the intentions of the then-deceased Cardinal Nicholas of Cusa approximately A.D. 1480. This was notably the Cusa who had prescribed the formation of the modern sovereign nation-state, with his *Concordancia Catholica*, and had not only founded modern European science, but defined the method of all competent science, afresh, with his *De Docta Ignorantia*, and with the work of such among his avowed followers as Leonardo da Vinci and Johannes Kepler. This same Cusa had recognized, from the aftermath of the conquest of Constantinople and the resulting breakup of the great ecumenical agreement forged at the Council of Florence, that European civilization was in a process of a new descent. Cusa had pointed his associates and followers to the importance of crossing the great oceans with the intent to renew European civilization from abroad. Christopher Columbus' voyage to the Americas was the explicit outcome of his adoption of Cusa's advice.

In the aftermath of Columbus' voyages of discovery intended to this end, what was to become our United States emerged, beginning, most emphatically, with the establishment of the Plymouth and later Massachusetts English colonies in 1620-1688 New England. This process in North America itself, assimilated something greater than the floods of immigrants from sundry parts of Europe; the best among the settlers brought with them a devotion to the greatest achievements of European civilization, but achievements largely freed from the oligarchical legacy's grip on the nations and culture of Old Europe.

Thus, our republic was founded as a constitutional nation-state under a Presidential system, rather than the crippled form of self-government represented by the parliamentary systems typical of western and central Europe to the present time. In matters bearing on the subject of scientific and related expressions of creativity, the most significant feature of specifically American republican culture, as distinct from the followers of the British East India Company, such as Judge Lowell, is the emphasis on the promotion of the scientific and related creativity of the typical citizen of what was to become our new republic.

Since that time, especially since the time of that February 1763 Peace of Paris which established the British East India Company as a privately controlled, Anglo-Dutch Liberal, financier empire, we in our U.S.A. have been divided, even in our scientific culture, between the patriotic tradition associated with Leibniz and the fraudulent, anglophile form of the Liberal tradition of Paolo Sarpi, as typified by the legacy of René Descartes and the hoaxster Isaac Newton.

Sarpi's Hoax

That much stated by way of general introduction, we now bring the discussion to the core of the matter.

The strategic problem, as defined by Paolo Sarpi's cultural policy, was to attempt to offset the effect of the creativity promoted by the strategic policies of such Cusa followers as Luca Pacioli, Leonardo da Vinci, Niccolò Machiavelli, and Johannes Kepler, by allowing a certain degree for technical innovations, but without allowing anything resembling the principle of creativity as exemplified by the discoveries of Cusa, Pacioli, Leonardo, and Kepler. To this end, whereas Sarpi had overthrown the authority of Aristotle, he replaced Aristotle with the raving, empiricist lunacy borrowed from the medieval William of Ockham.

On this account, we must see clearly both the agreement and disagreement between the philosophies of Aristotle and Ockham. Both, like Aristotle's follower Euclid, located knowledge within the limits of blind faith in sense-certainty, as did Sarpi's apologist René Descartes. The difference lay essentially in Sarpi's fostering innovation to the extent it did not lead to actually scientific knowledge and practice. With Sarpi, especially as his influence is expressed in Descartes and such Eighteenth-Century followers of Cartesian empiricism as de Moivre, D'Alembert, the hoaxster Euler, and Lagrange, or the hoaxster Augustin Cauchy later, algebraic and related mathematical formulas are substituted for the kinds of those universal principles of physical science which are typified, explicitly, by the work of Kepler, Fermat, Leibniz, (implicitly) Gauss, Bernhard Riemann, Max Planck, and Albert Einstein—in opposition to such fraudsters as mechanist Ernst Mach or the even worse set of followers of the purely evil Bertrand Russell.

In all cases of Sarpian empiricism and its modern positivist outgrowths, the assumed pre-existence of mere forms, becomes a general set of arbitrary assumptions of belief superseding the simpler set of a-priori definitions, axioms, and postulates of an essentially Aristotelean Euclidean geometry. In this way, as Descartes explicitly prescribes this modern empiricist form of so-called "scientific" irrationalism, no margin is permitted for the actual discovery of any actually universal principle, such as Kepler's uniquely original discovery of gravitation, of our universe.

What, according to Albert Einstein, distinguishes the quality of originality in Kepler, is the originality of Kepler's discovery of the evidence showing that his principle of universal gravitation is defined by the ironical juxtaposition of the human sensory apparatus' senses of sight-versus-(harmonically ordered) sound, exactly as Max Planck's discovery of the quantum principle remains the necessary alternative to the mechanistic hoax of the pathological so-called quantum mechanics of both mechanistic and Russellite types. Kepler develops the foundations of this crucial argument at the foundations of his general discovery in the opening section of his work on the principles of universal harmonics.

As Einstein emphasized, the locating of Kepler's work as the underlying practical-scientific foundation of modern mathematical physics, leads Einstein to emphasize that the universe is self-bounded, as by Kepler's harmonically-ordered principle of universal gravitation, and is therefore mathematically finite, but without external bounds.

The specific genius of Kepler's discovery on this account, is the crucially experimental form of the demonstration that neither sight nor sound underlies the principle of universal gravitation. Rather, gravitation, as discovered, uniquely, by no one but Kepler, is the primary discovery, in science in general, which shows us the means by which the individual human being's mind is able to discover principles which rule the evidence of the senses as if from outside and above.

This discovery, when recognized, as it must be, by any competent science classroom, leads us to a general notion of what we may term "scientific instrumentation." When we see that human sight and sound are merely instrumentation delivered in the package with the mortal human body, we are able to reach more broadly, into comprehension of a general theory of scientific instrumentation, under whose direction we recognize that the universe's efficient quality of existence is not in the form defined by the senses; but, that the senses perceive those shadows of reality which are adumbrations, rather than the actuality of universal principles. So, we proceed from our given senses, to the supplementary devices we recognize as instrumentation into the microphysical and cosmic domains.

The case is made sufficiently well in Kepler's opening sections of his ***Harmonies***. Sky Shields and his team, now addressing the crucial work of Riemann, have carried this into the direction of a study of the ironies explored jointly by Max Planck and by the Wolfgang Köhler of Köhler's ***The Mentality of Apes.***

These are the aspects of Tuesday evening's discussion which were not referenced in Wednesday morning's briefing lead.

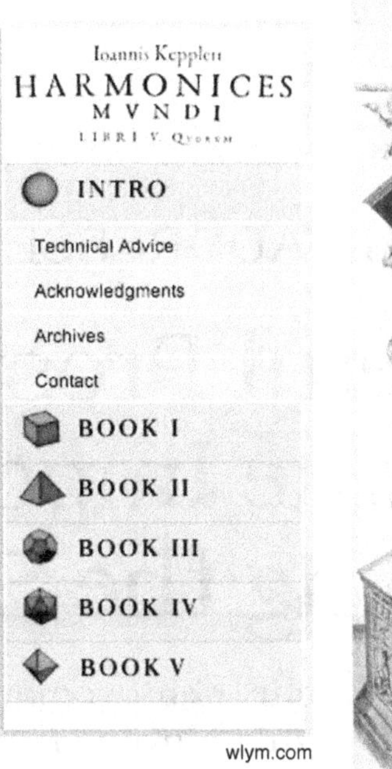

wlym.com

Johannes Kepler (1571-1630) gave modern science its first practicable, scientific conception of the astronomical universe. The illustrations here are from the LaRouche Youth Movement's "Basement" project on Kepler's Harmony of the World; *the LYM explicates this monumental work through the use of animated graphics and musical examples (www.wlym. com/~animations). The drawing is from Kepler's frontispiece to his 1627 Rudolphine Tables. It shows Copernicus and Tycho Brahe at the center, while Hipparchus and Ptolemy look on. On the base, the panel to the left shows Kepler himself, laboring by candlelight. The musical scales shown here are taken from Kepler's* Harmony, *and show the "tonalities" of the harmonic orbits of the planets (these can be heard on the website). Above is the major scale; below is the minor scale.*

On Hopeful Prospects for 2018 And the Impossibility of Keeping the Status Quo

by Helga Zepp-LaRouche, chairwoman of the German political party,
Civil Rights Movement Solidarity (BüSo)

Dec. 22—If, in times like these, you want to arrive at an adequate assessment of the situation we are in—the strategic and historical situation—it is imperative to see the world from different angles. You should not only look at the events as through a zoom lens, in which the very-small of German political correctness is inflated out of all proportion, but you should reflect on the world for a moment from German, then again from Chinese, Russian, American, African, and other perspectives.

It is perfectly obvious that none of the parties participating in the slow-moving exploratory talks on forming a new German government, has even attempted this approach, and that none of them has a vision of what the future of Germany should look like in ten, fifty, or one hundred years. And that has a paralyzing effect on public awareness in our country. Since the mainstream media, for their part, believe they have to determine which topics are newsworthy and which should not be covered, political discourse on matters of life-and-death importance hardly takes place in Germany, except in our own media, of course.

By far the biggest gap between the assumptions of

Schiller Institute

Helga Zepp-LaRouche

the majority of the population, and reality, concerns the image that most people have of China and of the Silk Road Initiative, which President Xi Jinping put on the international agenda more than four years ago. Only those who have been to China, or have been investing in, or trading with China, have an idea of the unprecedented success of the Chinese economic miracle and the largest infrastructure and development program in history. This is a program involving more than 70 countries that, thanks to this collaboration on a win-win basis, now participate in the "Spirit of the New Silk Road," that is, in an optimism that has been completely lost in Germany.

Most people have very little knowledge of China and are often influenced by the media's negative coverage, ranging from diffuse fears of "the yellow peril" to the idea of an autocratic system—without democracy or human rights—with an imperial claim to world power. The reality is quite different: China has undergone a tremendous transformation in recent years, transmuting itself, in a manner of speaking, into the Confucian-shaped opposite of the ten years of the Cultural Revolution, lifting 700 million people out of poverty. And it intends to enable the remaining 42 million still living in poverty to make a decent living by 2020.

In stark contrast to the mood in Germany, where most people think, for the first time, that future generations will be worse off, the absolute majority of the Chinese people are very optimistic about the future. According to Western surveys, 83% of the population of China is very satisfied with the government's policy, in contrast, for example, to about 42% in Germany.

When President Trump presented the new National Security Strategy report on Dec. 18, he attempted to mitigate its geopolitical orientation by deviating from the text, emphasizing that he wanted to build a strong partnership with Russia and China. But he still spoke of China and other states as competitors. The reaction from China was clear. Foreign Ministry spokeswoman Hua Chunying commented on Trump's speech at the ministry's regular press conference on Dec. 19, saying: "The development achievements scored by China are universally acknowledged and it is of no avail to attempt to distort the facts on the part of anyone or any country. No one and no country can stop the Chinese people from unwaveringly continuing following the path of socialism with Chinese characteristics and reaping greater achievements."

The self-confidence expressed in these formulations is typical of Chinese society today, and it has a real basis in the tremendous progress China has made in recent decades. For example, China has developed about 30,000 kilometers of high-speed railways, on which first-class trains run with a top speed 330 km per hour; a new model that can reach 400 km per hour speed has already been developed; and by 2020, China plans to have 50,000 kilometers of track and to have all major cities interconnected with high-speed rail.

Compare this with the embarrassing demonstrations of lost engineering skills at the opening of the high-speed rail route from Berlin to Munich—before Christmas, after 26 years of construction—when the train control system malfunctioned, or the saga of the new Berlin airport that is scheduled to open who knows when. While Germany's Transrapid high-speed monorail, with magnetic levitation, still does not run in Germany, it does in China. The same is the case with the inherently safe, high-temperature nuclear reactor de-

veloped in Germany, which is being built in China. The cost of the ill-considered transition out of nuclear must be borne by the consumer. And which of the parties represented in the Bundestag has a plan to help roughly the 20% of children living in poverty in Germany, to reach a good standard of living by 2020? Not to mention the results of the EU austerity policy in the Southern European countries, or the falling life expectancy in the United States.

In view of the obvious success of the Chinese model and the equally obvious disadvantages of our system, which only benefits the rich and leaves the poor with no hope of overcoming this state of affairs, would it not be advisable to consider objectively what China does better than we do? The Chinese are now absolutely confident that they have the superior economic and social model. And they do not want to export and impose this model by means of the Silk Road Initiative, but only to offer the benefits of win-win economic cooperation. President Xi Jinping has also proposed a completely new model of international cooperation between states having equal rights regardless of their size, with each having full respect for the other's sovereignty and self-determined social model. Xi speaks of humanity being a "community of common destiny," which implies the idea of one humanity coming before the interests of the individual nation. Should not everyone who cares about world peace be relieved and happy that, for the first time, a concept global governance is being proposed that overcomes geopolitics at the higher level of the common interest of the human species?

So how can one explain that the EU, the Bundestag parties (if they comment on the Chinese policy at all), most think tanks, and the mainstream media, stubbornly persist in using the categories of geopolitics, usually with the argument that the EU needs even more integration so it can assert itself "against" China, Russia, the United States, and so on?

The answer is prosaic. The permanent bureaucracies, as well as the EU and party establishments , owe their privileges to the monetarist system, which favors speculation at the expense of the common good. And since they are personally very well off materially, they are career-conditioned not to think outside the box of the existing system and to instinctively do everything to maintain the status quo. Ever since Chancellor Kohl upheld the principle that one must "sit out" problems—

that is, for over three and a half decades now—mediocrity has become the standard in Germany, which Angela Merkel, who refuses to look beyond the end of her nose and will only "take small steps" in politics, has brought to a new low.

This establishment proves to be utterly incapable of recognizing that preserving the status quo is impossible in times of such epoch-making upheavals as we are currently experiencing. The most clinical form of this denial can be seen in Hillary Clinton, who neither wants to accept the reasons for her election defeat nor the damage she and the "Democratic" Party are inflicting on the reputation of democracy through their participation in the coup attempt against President Trump.

Nevertheless, the forecast for 2018 looks fundamentally positive. While there are some serious threats, most notably the likelihood of a new financial crash worse than the one in 2008, the fact that the framework for a new economic and financial system already exists, in the form of the Silk Road Initiative and a real-economy banking system that includes institutions such as the AIIB, the New Silk Road Fund, and others, gives rise to optimism that the crisis can be mastered.

It is therefore more likely that the enormous economic benefits from cooperation with the Chinese policy—and that have long since been recognized by the countries of Asia, Africa, Latin America, Eastern and Central Europe, the Balkans, Southern Europe, Austria and Switzerland—can no longer be concealed. More and more people in Germany—the middle class, the people who feel left behind—will realize that the New Silk Road provides opportunities for all of humanity.

So, when we look out beyond the narrow confines of Germany and see the optimistic dynamics among the nations that are gripped by the "spirit of the New Silk Road," and understand that we are in the process of experiencing and shaping the dawn of a whole new era of humanity, then enthusiasm for the future will arise even in Germany.